DAIMLER COACHES IN COLOUR

JIM NEALE

FRONT COVER IMAGE: Coventry Cathedral with a Coventry coach (see page 73 for details). (Tom Moore, digitally coloured by Garry Luck)

BACK COVER IMAGE: A smart pair of Daimler Freeline coaches with contrasting Plaxton bodies in the fleet of Burwell & District Motor Service. UVE 101 is also shown on page 71, and LYG 398 on page 58. (Author)

TITLE PAGE IMAGE: A pair of preserved Blue Bus Daimlers, GNU 750 (page 15) and ORB 277 (page 20), posed together near Etwall Church when visiting home territory in September 1979. (David Stanier)

CONTENTS PAGE IMAGE: CF6 7131S, RU 8910, HALL LEWIS, C26D
Three of fifteen coaches (RU 8900–14) supplied to Shamrock & Rambler, Bournemouth in 1929. Photographed at the Daimler Service Centre, at Willesden in North London before delivery. (Tom Moore collection, digitally coloured by Garry Luck)

Published by Key Books
An imprint of Key Publishing Ltd
PO Box 100
Stamford
Lincs PE19 1XQ

www.keypublishing.com

The right of Jim Neale to be identified as the author of this book has been asserted in accordance with the Copyright, Designs and Patents Act 1988 Sections 77 and 78.

Copyright © Jim Neale, 2021

ISBN 978 1 913870 80 5

All rights reserved. Reproduction in whole or in part in any form whatsoever or by any means is strictly prohibited without the prior permission of the Publisher.

Typeset by SJmagic DESIGN SERVICES, India.

CONTENTS

Introduction	4
Chapter 1 – Front-Engined	5
Chapter 2 – Mid-Engined	33
Chapter 3 – Rear-Engined	81

INTRODUCTION

I first took an interest in Daimler coaches as a teenager as my local operator, Burwell & District Motor Service, ran a predominantly Daimler fleet. I have documented most of the various models for more than half a century and built up a comprehensive collection of photos of all types. When I realised that buses all had a chassis number, I started to keep my photographic records in numerical order and eventually filled in the gaps by pestering a sympathetic Daimler bus salesman at the Commercial Motor Show when I was 18 years old. At that time, I was a bus conductor for B&D and often volunteered to drive to Coventry to collect spare parts from the Daimler factory. With a contact made, I talked my way into the sales office and was allowed to copy the chassis numbers and vehicle details from official records, and so was able to assist the PSV Circle a few years later when they were compiling Daimler records.

I have self-published five books about buses and coaches that I have driven and been involved in. The last two being in full colour, as I think that black and white images are now out of date in the 21st century. I am fortunate to have found someone who is skilled in digital colourisation and has provided me with many colour images of vehicles that I had never seen in colour and, in some cases, of vehicles that no picture appeared to exist. Although Ian Allan have published books on Daimler buses and coaches in the past, they were all in black and white and covered the whole range. I hope that by concentrating on coaches, this book will appeal to a wider audience who are interested in coaches in general. I would like to acknowledge reference to the records of The Omnibus Society, PSV Circle and The Bus Archive as well as my own many contacts, extensive records and library. Thanks also to John Bennett for supplying scans from The Bus Archive and Martin Ingle for additional information and checking the final draft. Without the digital skills of Garry Luck, this book would not have been possible, also the many original photographers, who are acknowledged individually.

Vehicle details are shown in standard PSV Circle codes: Chassis type and number, Registration number, Body make, model, (number), F = Full-front, HD = Half-deck, C = Coach, DP = Dual-purpose, number of seats, door position, F = Front, C = Centre, R = Rear, D = Dual, T = Toilet.

CHAPTER 1
FRONT-ENGINED

There can be no doubt that the first Daimler bus evolved from the Company's success as a builder of large motor cars, or Horseless Carriages, as they were then known. Daimler produced the chassis, on which various coachbuilders mounted bodies built to customers' requirements. Many generations of Royalty specified Daimler motor cars and the Company was awarded the Royal Warrant which was proudly displayed above the Head Office Showroom at the Radford Works.

The Daimler Company had no need to put their name on the front of their vehicles, as the shiny fluted radiator shell had become a well-known symbol of passenger transport supremacy around the world. This trademark would remain on all vehicles produced with an exposed front-mounted radiator. Eventually, this was replaced by a stylish script which sometimes incorporated scalloped flutes in various styles to form a distinctive emblem to suit coachwork as designs advanced and radiator locations changed. The smooth-running Daimler engine driving through a fluid-flywheel to a pre-selector gearbox provided the base for many different styles of coachwork as shown in the following pages.

W 963
This CK type chassis with replica body similar to their first vehicle was built by Barton Transport to celebrate the Coronation of Queen Elizabeth II in 1953. An early example of bench seating which evolved into the more luxurious Charabanc as seen on the next page. It is seen here giving a ride to members of the PSV Circle from Colchester on a visit to Barton`s depot in 1967. Re-painted in the traditional Barton red/maroon/cream livery in the 1980s, it is now kept at the Barton Heritage Centre at Chilwell. (Author)

40 HP CHARABANC, FK 425
One of three vehicles new in 1913 to The Worcester Electric Traction Company. The folding roof with separate doors for each row of seats was an early form of motorised coach. They were subsequently pressed into military service during the First World War. (Tom Moore collection, digitally coloured by Garry Luck)

CF6 7247S, NH 9866, DUPLE, (1885), C24D
One of six (NH 9861–6) new in April 1930 to Allchin`s Luxury Coachways, Northampton, an old established company whose owners were related to the maker of traction engines of the same name. They operated holiday tours and regular express services to London, Great Yarmouth, Bournemouth, Torquay and various other coastal destinations. (Tom Moore collection, digitally coloured by Garry Luck)

CF6 7668S, VV 5, PARK ROYAL, C26D
The progression from normal-control to forward-control separated the driver from passengers in a half-cab and allowed two extra seats to be fitted. One of four (VV 5–8), new to Allchin in June 1930. The Road Traffic Act of 1930 introduced Road Service Licensing, which eventually led to the sale of Allchin`s Luxury Coachways to the United Counties Omnibus Company in December 1933 and most of the coaches continued in service in Tilling green/cream livery. (The Bus Archive, digitally coloured by Garry Luck)

ASSOCIATED DAIMLER, ADC 416A 416743, BR 6496
A brief joint venture between Daimler and AEC resulted in this Associated Daimler, new in April 1928 to Northern General with Hall Lewis bodywork. Re-bodied in 1979 with a Wyatt C30D replica body and roll-back canvas roof, known as 'The King of the Road', in yellow/maroon, it was rallied in the UK in the early 1980s. It was exported to the United States, then later returned to the United Kingdom and now owned and rallied by the ADC Group, Sheffield. It is seen here at the 2012 Llandudno Festival of Transport taking part in a road run around the Great Orme. (Keith Valla)

ASSOCIATED DAIMLER, ADC 423 423005, UP 632, SHORT Brothers, FC20FT
This luxurious coach was exhibited at the 1927 Commercial Motor Show at Olympia. Featuring a front saloon with 14 fixed seats, a kitchen and toilet were fitted amidships, and six individual armchairs were placed in the rear section. Registered in February 1928 by J Glenton Friars of Blaydon to launch a new coach service between Newcastle upon Tyne and London at a fare of £1 single, £1.15 shillings return. The service ran three times a week, with a refreshment break in Doncaster. This proved successful and several new Daimler CF6 coaches were ordered (UP 3232, page 12), allowing UP 632 to return to Daimler as a demonstrator, as seen here in what is thought to be a typical livery of the period. (Tom Moore collection, digitally coloured by Garry Luck)

CF6 7190L, HOYAL, C25FT, UP 3232
One of a pair (UP 3232–3) new to Glenton Friars North Road Coach Service in July 1929 and used on their successful route between Tyneside and London, which by then was operated daily. The two-man crew demonstrate the fully enclosed roof-mounted luggage lockers which were patented by the Hoyal Body Corporation. A second spare wheel and additional luggage lockers were incorporated in the sides of the coachwork. The service passed to United Automobile Services in 1932 and after five years of smoothly traversing the A1 trunk road, United had Northern Counties bus bodies fitted to the Daimler chassis and later AEC engines. (Tom Moore collection, digitally coloured by Garry Luck)

CF6 7196L, MT 3957
New to Webber Bros., Wood Green, London, (Empires Best) with Newns C31D body in May 1929. Acquired by Burwell & District Motor Service, Cambridgeshire in May 1935, fitted with new DUPLE (5525) C32F body as fleet no. 15, where it joined other Daimler CF6 buses with Willowbrook bodies bought new. To cope with wartime demands, W L Thurgood of Ware fitted 39 dual-purpose seats in May 1940. The Duple body was fitted to a new CVD6 chassis in 1947, registered FVE 526, which was in turn re-bodied with a new Plaxton body in 1949 (page 23). (Author's Collection, digitally coloured by Garry Luck)

COG5 10723, FOF 251
Chassis new to Birmingham Corporation with BRCW H30/24R body in 1939. The chassis was given a new lease of life by being lengthened and fitted with new BURLINGHAM Sunsaloon (4618) FC37F body for SS Motorways, Birmingham in July 1951. It passed to Butler`s Crimson Coaches, Henley-on-Thames, Oxfordshire in 1952. Albert Spiers took over Butler on retirement and later replaced the Gardner 5-cylinder engine with an AEC 6-cylinder 7.7 litre engine from an ex-Manchester Corporation CWA6, GNF 163, which improved performance, if not economy! It was sold to Lambert, Guildford in 1960 and scrapped by 1964. (Mike Wells Collection, digitally coloured by Garry Luck)

COG5-40 8485, GNU 750, WILLOWBROOK, (3208), C35F
New to Tailby & George, (Blue Bus Services), Willington, Derbyshire, fleet no. Dr 5 in May 1939. The fleet number indicates this is the fifth of its type. The previous four were fitted with dual-purpose seats. It was sold for preservation to Colin Shears, Exeter in July 1965. It then moved to John Horrocks, Derby, 1967, onto Barry Mapperson, Coventry, circa 1976, then to Jeffs Coaches, Helmdon, Northamptonshire in 1983. It was sold to Stephen Morris, (Quantock Motor Services), Somerset in November 2006 where it is seen here in the Devon village of Iddesleigh in October 2007. It was exported to Urnas, Kaunus, Lithuania in 2011 to promote a shopping centre with local registration EOU 585. (Martyn Hearson)

CVD6 17460, EVY 710, BARNABY, C35F
New in May 1950 to Edward Sheriff, (Reliance Motor Services), York in predominantly cream livery, which was reversed to mainly green by the time it was seen here outside the Rowntree factory in York in May 1966. Reliance was an old established company with a head office in York and depots at Helmsley and Sutton-on-the-Forest, where the company is still based, under new ownership. (Robin Jenkinson, digitally coloured by Garry Luck)

CVD6 15083, JTC 34, YORKSHIRE EQUIPMENT, C33F
New in June 1948 and one of several Daimler CVD6 coaches bought by W Robinson & Sons, Great Harwood, Lancashire soon after the war when established coachbuilders could not cope with demand. Robinsons had several chassis bodied by Plaxton, which went on to lead longer lives with other operators. They were also part of the Holdsworth & Hanson Group, who owned Broughton & Walker, also of Great Harwood and the Yorkshire Equipment Company of Bridlington, who built coach bodies for both companies. Due to shortages after the war, they used green un-seasoned timber in the framework, which resulted in most of these coaches being re-bodied in the early 1950s. JTC 34 received a full-front Plaxton Venturer II body (2121) FC35F with H Pemberton of Upton, Yorkshire in February 1953. (Tom Moore collection, digitally coloured by Garry Luck)

CVD6 17257, HWW 768, WILKS & MEADE, C33F
New in July 1949 to Tom Burrows & Sons, Wombwell, Yorkshire, who had also purchased similar coaches GWX 167–8 the previous year. Wilks & Meade were established in Leeds before the war and were owned by Wallace Arnold by the time this coach was built. The poor quality of materials resulted in short lives for some bodies, and most were re-built or re-bodied. It is seen here in August 1961, before withdrawal two years later. (Geoff Mills, digitally coloured by Garry Luck)

Front-Engined

CVD6 15913, HVE 402, WILKS & MEADE, FCL27/26RD

One of the three double-decker coaches supplied to Premier Travel, Cambridge, fleet no. 73 in 1950. Premier Travel was an old established East Anglian independent operator and pioneer of express coach services who had hoped to use these vehicles on long-distance routes but were thwarted by the Traffic Commissioners. They were, however, allowed to operate on the lengthy services from Suffolk to Kings Cross, London. HVE 401–3 were named 'County of Cambridge', 'West Suffolk' and 'Essex', respectively, and were the only double-deckers built by Wilks & Meade. The use of un-seasoned timber required extensive re-framing in Premier Travel's workshop. Premier Travel had previously purchased six half-cab coaches from Wilks & Meade on Leyland and Daimler chassis, possibly due to their connection with Wallace Arnold as booking agents across East Anglia. (Geoff Rixon, digitally coloured by Garry Luck)

CVD6 17375, ORB 277, DUPLE, (50201), C35F
New in July 1950 to Tailby & George, (Blue Bus Services), Willington Derbyshire, fleet no. Dr 12 in July 1950. After serving the well-known Daimler fleet for almost 20 years, the coach was sold to local enthusiast and Blue Bus historian David Stanier, Stretton, for preservation in March 1970. After ten years of restoration and participation in the local rally scene it passed to BAMMOT, Wythall Museum in July 1980. It is seen here at Willington Power Station on the Blue Bus Farewell tour on 18 August 1973. (Terry Walker)

CVD6 13463, BCF 59, DUPLE, (47010), C35F
New in December 1947 to Morley's Grey Coaches, West Row, Suffolk. The Ministry of Supply allocated chassis to operators in the post-war period and this Daimler joined several AEC Regal coaches and was soon sold to nearby Burwell & District in March 1949 for £3,800. Ironically, B&D were allocated an AEC Regal chassis in November 1945, which was not delivered until May 1947, where it joined a fleet of mainly Daimler half-cabs. BCF 59 was withdrawn in February 1957, passing via a dealer to another Morley, (Whittlesey Bus Service), Whittlesey, Cambridgeshire. (Author, digitally altered and coloured by Garry Luck)

CVD6 13616, FVE 559, HARRINGTON, (126), C32F
New in June 1947 to Burwell & District Motor Service, Cambridgeshire. Due to the post-war shortage of materials, a painted radiator was fitted. A new chrome radiator shell was supplied by Daimler a year later at a cost of £49.5 shillings. A similar Harrington-bodied coach, GVE 781, arrived at Burwell in December 1948 and both eventually passed to Harry Webster of Pattishall, Northamptonshire where they served for a couple of years on contracts in the early 1960s.
(Author's Collection, digitally altered and coloured by Garry Luck)

CVD6 14197, FVE 526
Marshalls of Cambridge transferred the 1935 Duple body from Daimler CF6 MT 3957 (page 13) on to the new chassis which entered service in June 1947. In April 1949, a new PLAXTON (290) C32F body was fitted and served B&D until June 1962. A similar Plaxton-bodied coach was purchased by B&D in March 1950. The chassis of HVE 426 cost £1,910 and the body £1,700. This was the last half-cab coach run by B&D and was withdrawn in September 1963 and eventually broken up the following year. A third Plaxton-bodied Daimler was acquired second-hand in April 1951. HTD 76 had been new to W Robinson & Sons of Great Harwood in 1947 and left Burwell in February 1957 to join the fleet of Wessex Coaches in Bristol. (Geoff Mills, digitally altered and coloured by Garry Luck)

CVD6 14525, BMS 415, BURLINGHAM, (2883), C33F, Fleet no. D20
One of a batch of 29 (D2–30) that was new to Walter Alexander, Falkirk, in March 1948. D1 had been new in May 1947 and D31–5 followed in March 1949. When Alexander split into regional companies in May 1961, the coaches were dispersed throughout the group. Four of this batch were transferred to Alexander (Northern) and remained in service until 1970, when three of them eventually passed into preservation and survive in varying conditions. BMS 415 is seen here at the Dunbar Bus Rally in 1983. (Geoff Stainthorpe)

CVD6 17407, JVC 4, BURLINGHAM, (4507), C33F
The first of four consecutively numbered coaches for Red House Motor Services, Coventry, new in May 1950. JVC 4 and 7 both passed to Leon Motor Services, Finningley, Nottinghamshire in January 1960. They were both withdrawn in 1966. JVC 4 is seen here in July 1963. Leon were keen Daimler operators, with three other CVD6 coaches bought new and another second-hand. They also ran a CVD6 double-decker on their stage-carriage route in to Doncaster and purchased a new Burlingham Seagull-bodied Freeline in 1954, PNN 788. (Geoff Mills, digitally coloured by Garry Luck)

CVD6 16263, KGY 929, TRANS-UNITED, FC32F
One of a pair (KGY 928–9) supplied to Charles Rickards of Paddington, London in 1949 in a maroon livery which carried the Royal Warrant. The first one was re-bodied by Duple in 1956, but this coach passed to Kildare Coaches, Adwick-le-Street, near Doncaster, Yorkshire in November 1959 where it joined a selection of other Daimler half-cab and full front coaches. Photographed here on withdrawal at Carcroft depot in July 1963. (Les Flint, John Law Collection)

CVD6 13611, DUX 655, METALCRAFT, FC33F
One of a pair (DUX 654–5) with ACB C33F bodies new to Smiths, (Eagle Coachways), Trench, Shropshire in March 1948. Both vehicles were subject to various body swaps, which resulted in DUX 655 receiving a new Metalcraft body in March 1950. The current owner acquired the coach for preservation in April 1974 and has rallied it extensively ever since, as seen here at the Showbus Rally, on Long Marston Airfield, Warwickshire in September 2013. (Michael Jefferies)

CVD6 17624, MTJ 843, SAMLESBURY, FC33F
One of three bodies built on CVD6 chassis, new in 1950 as an un-registered demonstrator. Offered to Burwell & District by Daimler for £3,500 in March 1951 but they declined. First registered and sold to H Platt (Bromley Cross Hire Service), Bolton in April 1951, passing to E Sheriff, (Reliance Motor Services), York in December 1952. Seen here at their Terminus in Exhibition Square, about to head to Helmsley, with Duple-bodied Daimler Freeline JDN 712 arrived behind, still in demonstration colours in October 1958. Both would later be re-painted in the predominantly green livery, as seen on page 16. MTJ 843 was withdrawn in June 1966. (John Cockshott, The Bus Archive, digitally coloured by Garry Luck)

CVD6 17398, MCE 201, HEAVER, FC35C
One of several stock chassis bodied by Heaver and sold as complete coaches by Daimler. Burwell & District Motor Service had already purchased new Plaxton-bodied Freelines in 1952 and 1953 and were offered this 'slightly soiled' coach at the special price of £3,300 in October 1953. It was returned to the Heaver works at Durrington in Wiltshire to be re-painted cream/brown. A radio was fitted at a cost of £58.15s.6d and the new coach was first registered in February 1954. Sold in December 1961 to A M Parkin, (Luxicoaches), Borrowash, Derbyshire, it then moved to Harry Webster, Pattishall, Northamptonshire in 1965, who ran it for six months before eventual scrapping. (Official Daimler photo, digitally coloured by Garry Luck)

CVD6 16078, OOC 100, BURLINGHAM SEAGULL, (5415), FC35F
The first of a trio of identical coaches supplied to Smiths Imperial Coaches, Sparkbrook, Birmingham in January 1954. It is surprising that Seagull bodies were still being built on front-engined chassis in 1953, when they were available on the underfloor-engined Freeline with 41 seats by then. Smiths Imperial did purchase a Freeline, but not until 1956. (RHP 774, page 60). OOC 100/300 passed to Kildare Coaches, Adwick-le-Street, Yorkshire in April 1962, where OOC 100 is seen withdrawn in June 1964, OOC 300 lasted another year. (Geoff Mills, digitally coloured by Garry Luck)

CVD6 18469, LBX 200, DUPLE, (1051/302), FC35F
New to Dan Jones, Carmarthen, fleet no. 10 in March 1955. This is the highest chassis number allocated to a CVD6 coach and possibly the last new one to enter service, although Dan Jones acquired a 1947 chassis that had originally carried a Yorkshire Yacht Building body for Robinson of Great Harwood, HTD 75 (see similar JTC 34 on page 17) and had a new Duple FC35F body fitted in March 1956, re-registered MTH 636, fleet no. 9. LBX 200 was sold to Pulham & Sons, Bourton-on-the-Water, Gloucestershire and is seen here in their yard in September 1971. Pulham's also bought one of only two Daimler CVD6 coaches to be bodied by Yeates of Loughborough (KAD 906). They also ran an early Daimler Freeline (PDD 472, page 53). (Andrew Harvey-Adams)

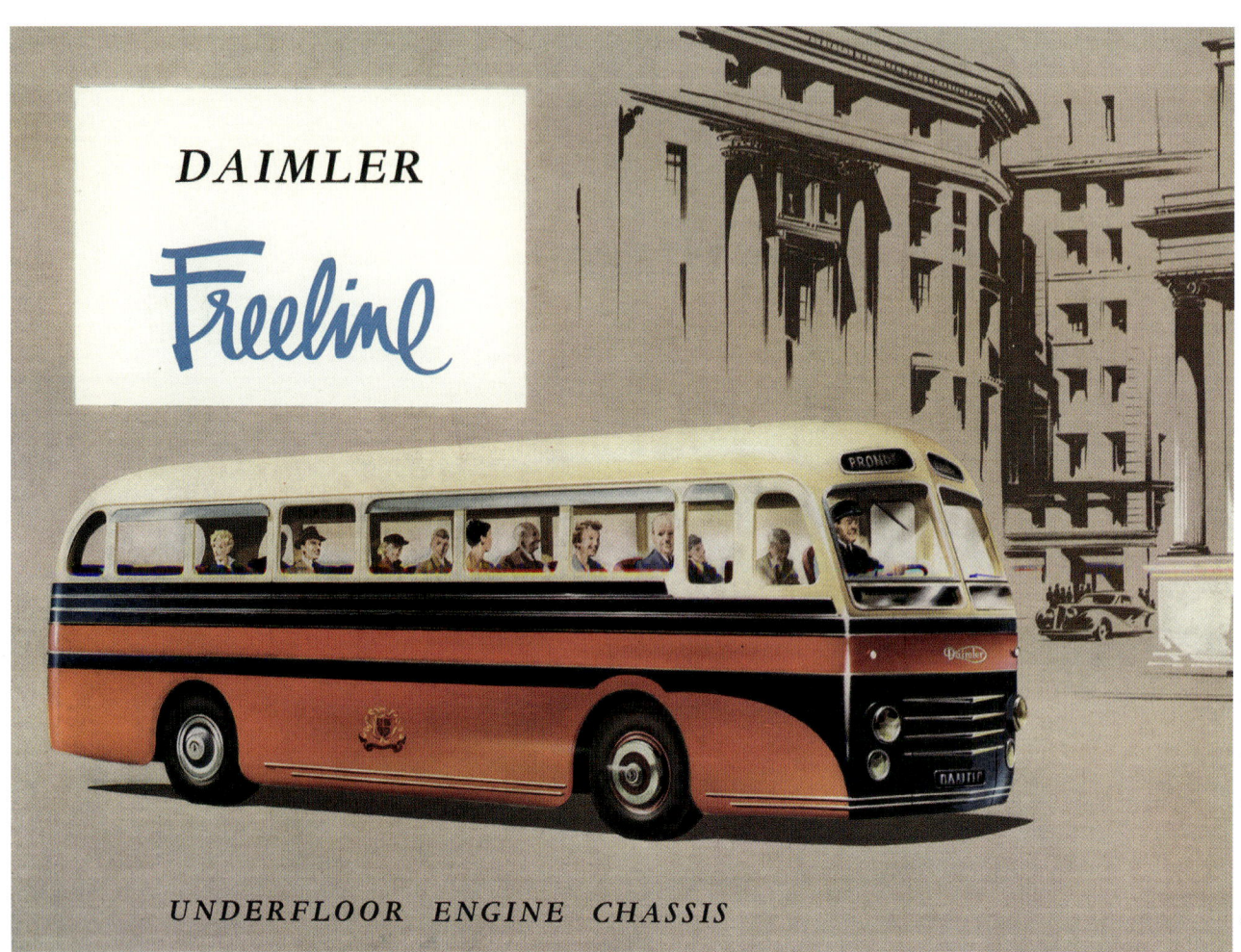

D650HS 25002
The coach that never was! This chassis was intended to be bodied by Duple as a demonstrator, but instead it was used as a prototype for road testing. This artist's impression of a Duple Roadmaster could have been commissioned with the intended use in mind and was used on the cover of a Freeline sales brochure. No Roadmaster bodies were mounted on Daimler chassis, and they became better known as Dinky Toys and, more recently, Oxford Diecast models rather than as real coaches.
(The Bus Archive)

CHAPTER 2
MID-ENGINED

Daimler had enjoyed considerable success with their front-engined coaches in the post-war travel boom. Many coach operators chose Daimler chassis as a prestige marque, which was well known for giving a smooth ride, where economy was not the main consideration. Most of their competitors had introduced underfloor-engined coaches and the Coventry product was known as the Freeline, the first Daimler chassis to be named. Two CV series chassis had been fitted with horizontal engines to test mechanical components, one the Daimler 10.6 litre and the other a Gardner 8.4 litre engine, before new purpose-built experimental chassis were constructed. Intensive testing of the Daimler-engined chassis included long road tests accompanied by the trade press, who were impressed by the performance of this heavy, powerful chassis. The first chassis was sent to HV Burlingham at Blackpool in March 1951 to be fitted with the popular Seagull body, as shown on the next page.

D650HS 25000, LKV 218, BURLINGHAM Seagull, (4850), C37C
New in 1951 as a demonstrator on trade plates. Registered in April 1952, it was loaned to Burwell & District Motor Service for a week in June to cover for delay in delivery of their first Freeline. Exhibited in the demonstration park at the 1952 Commercial Motor Show at Earls Court, where several other Freelines were displayed. Sold to Harman's Motor Services, Wolverhampton in February 1953, who had also purchased a similar coach new (KDA 555) in May 1952. It was later owned by Holt, Oldham, H Cooper, Gilesgate Moor, Co. Durham and Brookside Coaches, Deeping St James, Lincolnshire, and finished up as a band bus with a group in Norwich, Norfolk. (The Bus Archive, digitally coloured by Garry Luck)

D650HS 25066, LWR 840, BURLINGHAM Seagull, (4872), C39C
New to W Pyne & Sons, Starbeck, Harrogate, Yorkshire in July 1952. One of three Seagull bodies bought by this regular Daimler customer on Freeline chassis, Pynes were joint operators on the J16 express coach route between Harrogate and Blackpool, where this coach is parked in the Coliseum coach station. (John Kaye)

D650HS 25006, NAL 783, BURLINGHAM Seagull, (5201), C41C
New to W Gash & Sons, Newark, Nottinghamshire, fleet no. DO 7 in July 1952. Gash were long-standing Daimler customers and had purchased new CF6 and COG5 models before the war, followed by three CVD6 coaches and nine CVD6 double-deckers. Coaches were also used on stage carriage work and NAL 783 is seen here departing from Huntingdon Street Bus Station, Nottingham, duplicating one of Gash`s Massey-bodied Daimler CVD6 double-deckers on the service to Newark in August 1961. (Roger Cox)

D650HS 25005, NAL 782, BURLINGHAM Seagull, (5200), C41C
New to W Gash & Sons, Newark, Nottinghamshire, fleet no. DO 6 in May 1952. Sold to Trent Concrete for staff transport by 1968 and seen here back in Gash`s yard at Bowbridge Road for a visit from the Colchester branch of the PSV Circle on 1 May 1969, the year that Gash celebrated their Golden Jubilee. (Author)

D650HS 25279, NLR 848, BELLHOUSE HARTWELL Landmaster IV, C32C
One of eight luxury touring coaches (NLR 711–6, 848–9), it was new to Blue Cars Continental Coach Cruises, a member of the British Electric Traction Company, London in June 1953. An unusual feature was the outward opening hinged passenger door; they were the only bodies of this make to be mounted on Freeline chassis. When their touring days were over, they soon found new owners among independent operators. (Alan Broughall, digitally altered and coloured by Garry Luck)

Mid-Engined

D650HS 25009, UHY 211, HEAVER New Mark, C41C
New to Monarch Coaches, Bristol in May 1955. Heaver was a small coachbuilder, based in Durrington, Wiltshire but only bodied two Freelines, both of different styles, with this one based on the Burlingham Seagull design, which caused an adverse reaction from the Blackpool coachbuilder. Seen here at Victoria Coach Station on 10 June 1961 and withdrawn by Monarch in June 1964. (John Kaye)

D650HS 25027, MDU 600, BURLINGHAM Seagull, (5062), C41C
The first of six similar coaches for Red House Motor Services, Coventry delivered in July 1952. MKV 4–6 followed in 1953 and OKV 601–2 in 1954. The five later coaches were designated Seagull II and featured the double wing moulding separated by a concave swaged panel, as seen on some later Seagulls and illustrated on the next page. Red House were loyal to local maker Daimler and had previously owned CVD6 coaches and would later operate two Roadliners. (Official Daimler photo, digitally coloured by Garry Luck)

D650HS 25257, FHS 883, BURLINGHAM Seagull II, (4976), C37C
New to McKelvie, Barrhead, Renfrewshire in March 1953. McKelvie sold their coaching interests to R Dickson, Dundee in April 1955 and continued with their haulage operations for many years. This is the livery thought to have been carried when new, in contrast to the brown/red/cream of McKelvie's lorries. It is recorded as hired to Wallace Arnold from dealer Stanley Hughes from July to October 1956, then owned by Gosling, Gomersal from June 1957 to June 1969. (Official Daimler photo, digitally altered and coloured by Garry Luck)

D650HS 25013, KDA 581, METALCRAFT, C43C
New to Don Everall, Wolverhampton in June 1952. One of the only four Freelines to be bodied by Metalcraft (KDA 477–8, 581–2). Don Everall had several subsidiary companies and coaches moved between them and the main fleet, which made identity difficult, so it is possible that none of these four coaches actually carried the usual Everall colours as seen here. In fact, KDA 581 is recorded as passing to Everall subsidiary Black & White, Bilston in July 1952. A new division was formed under Don Everall (Stourbridge) in June 1957, and three months later, the coach passed to Bryn Melyn Motor Services, Llangollen, Denbighshire where it stayed until August 1964, when it was sold to V Hughes, Buckley, Flintshire. (Ken Swallow, digitally altered and coloured by Garry Luck)

D650HS 25015, LDA 721, MANN EGERTON, HDC26/24F
New to Don Everall, Wolverhampton in May 1953. The only one of 20 half-decker coaches built to be mounted on a Freeline chassis. The interlaced seating was designed and patented by Crellin-Duplex, enabling 50 seats to be provided within 30ft overall length, built under licence by Mann Egerton of Norwich. After changing hands several times, it was eventually scrapped in 1966.
(Digitally coloured from a brochure, which affects the quality, by Garry Luck)

D650HS 25035, EBV 282, DUPLE Ambassador, (118/1), C41C
One of a pair (EBV 282–3) new to Lewis Cronshaw, Hendon, London in May 1953, they were the only bodies of this style to be built on Freeline chassis. Sold to Prance Coaches, Cardiff in May 1961, and later owned by Bowden, Carlisle in 1964. Cronshaw had also purchased four CVD6 half-cabs in 1947, all with locally built Duple bodies. (The Bus Archive, digitally coloured by Garry Luck)

D650HS 25062, FCB 601, DUPLE Elizabethan, (200/2), C41C
The first of another pair for Lewis Cronshaw (FCB 601–2). Exhibited on the Daimler stand at the 1954 Commercial Motor Show, it was then entered in the First British Coach Rally at Clacton-on-Sea in April 1955. The following year it appeared in the first event held at Brighton. Later, it ran with Essex coach operators Cedric, Wivenhoe, Vines, Great Bromley and Brooks, Weeley.
(The Bus Archive, digitally coloured by Garry Luck)

D650HS 25040, KVE 166, PLAXTON Venturer, (1885), C41C
New to Burwell & District Motor Service in July 1952, this is the first of six Freelines to be operated by this loyal Daimler customer. Detailed documentation on this coach reveals that the chassis was ordered in July 1951 at a cost of £2,180 and the body was ordered in November, costing £2,316. Delivery was delayed due to a shortage of materials. The coach was one of three Freelines entered in the First British Coach Rally at Clacton-on-Sea in April 1955. It was withdrawn in 1965 and scrapped locally. (Author's Collection, digitally coloured by Garry Luck)

Mid-Engined

D650HS 25068, JRP 750, PLAXTON Venturer, (1884), C41C
This coach was completed by Plaxton in February 1953, a result of a cancelled order for an unknown operator and offered for sale in Commercial Motor by Comberhill Motors from June–October 1953 for £4,650 in cream/green for immediate delivery. It was sold to Thistle Services Ltd, Upper Benefield, Northamptonshire in December 1953. Thistle ran an express service from the Midlands to Scotland which passed to Barton/Robin Hood in 1955. The coach was sold to Meikle & McRae, Lesmahagow in 1956 and advertised for sale in 1963 by a Scottish dealer for £500, with a 'rough engine'. (Geoff Mills, digitally altered and coloured by Garry Luck)

D650HS 25041, CTS 256, PLAXTON Venturer II, (2004), C39C
Exhibited on the Plaxton stand at the 1952 Commercial Motor Show, it was delivered to R Dickson Junior, Dundee in November 1952, fleet no. 5. Built to a luxurious specification for Dickson`s Continental Tours, special features included fold-out steps from the front off-side emergency door for kerb access. It was advertised for sale in January 1953 at £5,400, but eventually entered service in February 1953. Dickson's Tours later sold out to Wallace Arnold Tours in 1963. (The Bus Archive, digitally coloured by Garry Luck)

ABOVE LEFT: CTS 256 passed to Heaps Tours, Leeds in March 1956, later passing to C W Blankley, (Gem Coaches), Colsterworth, Lincolnshire with 41 seats. Moving further south to Miller Brothers at Foxton, Cambridgeshire in October 1964, where it stayed for a year. (The Bus Archive, digitally altered and coloured by Garry Luck)

ABOVE RIGHT: D650HS 25059, HBO 700, PLAXTON Venturer II, (2141), C39C
One of a pair (HBO 699–700) new to E R Forse, Cardiff in April 1953. Forse was taken over by Western Welsh in April 1956 and the pair were withdrawn in 1962. (Author's Collection)

RIGHT: D650HS 25251, LCE 800, PLAXTON Venturer II, (2127), C41C
To ensure early delivery, a second Freeline chassis was ordered and delivered to Plaxton in January 1953. The price had increased to £2,445, and the body to £2,523. LCE 800 was delivered to Burwell in March, in good time to enter service in May 1953. After 14 years sterling service, it was part-exchanged for a Harrington-bodied AEC Reliance with a £50 allowance, driven to Loughborough on trade plates and subsequently scrapped. (Author)

D650HS 25173, VDH 742, DUPLE Elizabethan, (200/4), C41C
One of three Freelines new to Central Coachways, (Walsall), Staffordshire in July 1955 (VDH 740–2). Central was a subsidiary of Walsall Co-operative Society. The trio were built for stock by Duple, and so were fitted with various styles of side moulding to their Elizabethan bodies. VDH 742 shows how the different application of green and black on the base cream livery compares with VDH 741 (opposite). It was later owned by Garner's Coaches, Ealing, London W5. (Official Daimler photo, digitally altered and coloured by Garry Luck)

D650HS 25022, VDH 741, DUPLE Elizabethan, (200/9), C41C
New to Central Coachways, (Walsall) in July 1955. It was later owned by C E Lewis, Pailton, Rugby, Warwickshire, from January 1958 to July 1968. Lewis also ran several other second-hand Daimler coaches, including Burlingham Seagull-bodied Freeline, HNV 322, which had been new to Samuel Walters of Helmdon, Northamptonshire in 1952. (Official Daimler photo, digitally altered and coloured by Garry Luck)

D650HS 25051, VDH 740, DUPLE Elizabethan, (200/6), C41C
New to Central Coachways, (Walsall) in July 1955. Initially sold to Don Everall, (dealer), Wolverhampton in February 1959, it then passed to Da Costa, (Gatehouse Coaches), London N7 the following month. It went next to W L Handford, Mile Oak, Staffordshire in April 1960, then moved locally to S B James, Tamworth in January 1961. The next owner was Priory Coaches, Gosport, Hampshire in March 1962, before passing to W H Foster & Son, (Avalon Coaches), Glastonbury, Somerset in January 1964, where it joined similar ex-demonstration Freeline, PDD 472 (page 53). (John Kaye)

OPPOSITE: D650HS 25074
Originally fitted with a HARRINGTON Courier (1140) C41C body, it was exhibited on the Thomas Harrington stand as TH 1953 at the 1952 Commercial Motor Show in the colours of Shearings Tours, Oldham. The body was transferred to a Leyland Royal Tiger chassis and registered NVM 136 before entering the Shearings fleet. The Freeline chassis was then sent to Hendon, where it received a DUPLE Elizabethan (200/1) C41C body. It is seen here with Daimler CVG6 demonstrator PHP 220 in Coventry Corporation colours outside Earls Court at the 1954 Commercial Motor Show. The double-decker was sold to Burwell & District Motor Service in March 1956.
(John Gillham, digitally coloured by Garry Luck)

ABOVE RIGHT: Pulham's Coaches, of Bourton-on-the-Water, Gloucestershire had several CVD6 coaches and ordered a new Freeline coach (25078), but instead took the demonstrator, which was registered PDD 472 in May 1955. They advertised it for sale in March 1960 with 72,000 miles on the clock for £2,500 but continued to run it until February 1961. It was sold to Stanley Bingley, Hemsworth, Yorkshire the following month. It returned south to W H Foster & Son, (Avalon Coaches), Glastonbury, Somerset in October 1962, where it joined VDH 740 (page 51). (John Kaye)

RIGHT: It was sold to a Scout Troop in North London in May 1973 who then encountered transmission trouble which resulted in it being towed to the British Leyland Service Centre at Aldenham. Found to be uneconomic to repair, it was acquired by Burwell & District for spares and towed to Burwell in April 1974. After removal of vital organs, the shell joined NVE 1 (page 55) on a farm at Lode Fen, where it was broken up for scrap by a B&D driver, Brian Camps, who had steered it behind the tow-truck from Aldenham, and is seen here admiring the coach upon arrival at Burwell. Brian was also a Daimler enthusiast and had driven B&D Freelines for longer than the Author. Sadly, he passed away in May 2021, age 82, and was unable to see the restoration of NVE 1, or this book. (Author)

D650HS 25249, ROM 901, DUPLE Elizabethan, (200/12), C41C
New to the Dunlop Rubber Company, Birmingham in July 1955. From the body number it is obvious that this coach is the last Elizabethan-bodied Freeline, and one of several chassis that were cancelled orders sent to Hendon by Daimler, who sold them as complete vehicles, probably at competitive prices. (Official Daimler photo, digitally altered and coloured by Garry Luck)

D650HS 25185, NVE 1, WILLOWBROOK, 54196, C41C
This coach was exhibited on the Willowbrook stand at the 1954 Commercial Motor Show but did not enter service with Burwell & District Motor Service until March 1955. The chassis cost £2,350 and the body £2,565. This was the only centre entrance body built by Willowbrook on a Freeline chassis, although similar designs were built on various other chassis. The Author drove this coach several times after passing his PSV test in August 1970 until it was withdrawn from service in March 1971. After mechanical units had been removed, it was towed to Lode Fen and used as a store shed for many years. The registration was sold in 1976 and ATW 528A was allocated but not carried. It was rescued by Owen Edge in April 2019 for intended eventual restoration. (Official Willowbrook photo, digitally coloured by Garry Luck)

D650HS 25063, RTG 572, DUPLE Elizabethan, (200/7), C41C
New to S A Bebb, Llantwit Fardre, Glamorganshire, South Wales in May 1955. Despite extensive research I have been unable to find any information on this coach, and so commissioned a digital image of what is thought to have been Bebb's livery of the period. It was sold to A McGuigan, (Maxhire), Little Hulton, Lancashire in September 1962. (Official Daimler photo, digitally altered and coloured by Garry Luck)

D650HS 25014, KDA 582, METALCRAFT, C43C
The last of the four supplied new to Don Everall, Wolverhampton, (page 42) in 1952. The Everall Group controlled various companies, including Cooper & Victor of Wollaston, Worcestershire where this coach arrived in March 1956. It is seen here at Llandudno in August 1956, before passing to Castle Coaches, Birmingham in October 1957 and a couple of other owners before withdrawal in 1962. (Ken Swallow, digitally coloured by Garry Luck)

D650HS 25189, LYG 398, PLAXTON Venturer II, (2162), C41C
Fitted with glazed quarter lights, this coach was new to J W Kitchin & Sons, Pudsey, Yorkshire in April 1953. A good second-hand buy at £2,985 by Burwell & District Motor Service in April 1957 it was then scrapped in December 1967. Kitchin's also had a similar body, with less cove glazing on an AEC Regal IV chassis, registered LYG 399, which also passed through the ownership of several East Anglian operators. (Author's Collection, digitally altered and coloured by Garry Luck)

ABOVE LEFT and ABOVE RIGHT: D650HS 25178, LWT 704, HARRINGTON Wayfarer, (1109), C41C
New to J W Kitchin & Sons, Pudsey, Yorkshire in July 1952. Coachbuilder Thomas Harrington of Hove only bodied two Freelines, the Courier (mentioned on page 53) and this Wayfarer with their trademark Dorsal Fin at the rear end. Kitchin would later sell their coaching interests to Wallace Arnold in 1959. (The Bus Archive, digitally coloured by Garry Luck)

RIGHT: Sold to W Everett & Son, (United Services), South Kirkby, Yorkshire in November 1955. (Richard Simons)

D650HS 25181, RHP 774, DUPLE Elizabethan, (200/11), C41C
This chassis was another cancelled order that was bodied by Duple and became a Daimler demonstrator in July 1955, hence the Coventry registration. It was sold almost immediately to Smiths Imperial Coaches, Sparkbrook, Birmingham. Similar coach SOB 49 was also sold to another Birmingham coach operator, Newtons Coach Services of Perry Barr in July 1955. Smiths had previously bought a trio of new Burlingham-bodied CVD6 coaches in 1954 (OOC 100, 200, 300, page 30). (Official Daimler photo, digitally altered and coloured by Garry Luck)

ABOVE LEFT: D650HS 25016, RVM 37, DUPLE Elizabethan, (200/5), C41C
New to North Manchester Coaches in June 1955. It moved south to H H & J Say, Gloucester in 1958, then passed via a local dealer to P & D Lock, (Knight of the Road Coaches), Eastington, Gloucestershire in 1962, before it arrived at Spath, Staffordshire in July 1964. Here it received fleet no. 19 and the distinctive livery of John Stevenson's Yellow Bus Service, which it retained when driven to Burwell in August 1969. The engine and gearbox were fitted to B&D Freeline UVE 101 (page 71), and the remains were scrapped. (Author)

ABOVE RIGHT: D650HS 25061, RRW 700, DUPLE Elizabethan, (200/8), C41C
The third and final Daimler coach delivered to the Coventry & Warwickshire Hospital Saturday Fund in July 1955. It was sold to C W Brown & Son, (Witch Coaches), Warboys, Huntingdonshire in March 1968. It then passed to Rugg, Great Easton, Leicestershire in August 1968. Both coaches on this page were acquired direct from Daimler, who had surplus chassis bodied by Duple in plain cream, which was retained by the original owners as seen in this image. (D Gooding)

D650HS 25187, LGA 405, DUPLE Coronation Ambassador, (124/1), C30CT
This splendid coach was exhibited on the Duple stand at the 1952 Commercial Motor Show. This must have been one of the best appointed Freelines in the UK, joining a fleet of Burlingham Seagull-bodied AEC and Leyland coaches on the overnight service between Glasgow and London operated by Northern Roadways. With only 30 passenger seats, a toilet and refreshment facilities were provided at the rear of the coach along with a double seat for the second driver and hostess, who served hot drinks and pre-packed food to the passengers en route. Due to licensing restrictions, the service ended in 1956 and the coach was thought to have been used on tours until passing to Gillard's, Normanton, Yorkshire with increased seating capacity. It was operated by Leonard Carter, Kirkheaton, Yorkshire from December 1959 until April 1965. (The Bus Archive, digitally coloured by Garry Luck)

D650HS 25201, RFM 700, DUPLE Coronation Ambassador, (151/1), C41C
The 'Coronation' name related to the crowning of Queen Elizabeth II. This was new to George Taylor, Chester, in May 1953. Maybe the order was placed after seeing LGA 405 at Earls Court the previous September, as there were only two of these Coronation Ambassador bodies fitted to Freelines. It moved across the Welsh border to Huball, Wrexham in March 1965. It then went south to Williams, Gwaun-cae-Gurwen, South Wales in September 1970, where the Author tracked it down on 14 June 1972. He found that it had been withdrawn, the reason made obvious by the arc of flywheel fluid sprayed across the soft fluffy roof lining above the open inspection floor hatch. (Author)

D650HS 25410, FL-21-41, ALFREDO CAETANO
New to Isidoro Duarte, Povoa da Galega, Portugal in November 1954 with 35 bus seats, the flamboyantly styled body was extensively re-built to a more restrained style in 1971 and fitted with 43 coach seats but retained the front and rear doors, as seen here in July 1977. (Ian Charlton)

ABOVE LEFT: D650HS 25557, EG-24-16, ALFREDO CAETANO, DP43D
New to Eduardo Cabanelas, Felgueiras, Portugal in July 1956 in a similar style to the previous page. Also extensively re-built and fitted with 43 coach seats in 1973 for Auto Viacao Landim, Felgueiras when seen here in May 1978. (Mike Fenton)

ABOVE RIGHT: The chassis was re-built with an AEC engine and axles and a new MOTA DP47D body fitted in 1984, creating what could be called a 'Freeliance'! (Ian Charlton)

RIGHT: D650HS 25699, LC-76-11, MARTINS & CAETANO, DP43D
New to VM de Carnaxide, Portugal, fleet no.15 in August 1958. It was re-bodied by Salvador Caetano in September 1968, with the same seating configuration in a design similar to coaches imported to the UK by the Alf Moseley Group. (Bryan Bareham)

D650HS 25698, LC-46-08, CASTRO-REIS, C43D
New to Camionetas Nova Lusa, Sacavem, Portugal, fleet no. 3 in July 1958. It was re-bodied by Alfredo Caetano and fitted with a Leyland engine in March 1968 with Correia, Charlim & Vinagre, Ilhavo, fleet no. 4 when seen here in May 1979 sporting a custom-made DAIMLER name plate. (Ian Charlton)

D650HS 25669, BD-56-07, ALFREDO CAETANO, DP43D
New to Auto Mondinense, Mondim do Basto, Portugal, fleet no.12 in November 1957. Seen here in May 1979, the ornate coachwork would be replaced by a new UTIC B38D bus body in 1981. (Ian Charlton)

OPPOSITE: Daimler had sales agents worldwide, so achieved more sales of Freeline chassis abroad than at home. The State of Israel required additional vehicles in 1957 in preparation for the celebrations of the decade in 1958. Leyland was the predominant supplier but 20 Freeline chassis arrived in 1957 (D650HS 25670–89). Ten were bodied by MERKAVIM as B32T buses, entering service in August. The other ten carried more luxurious HAARGAS C43D bodies for EGGED, the largest transport operator in Israel. They entered service in the spring of 1958, in time to transport tourists celebrating the tenth anniversary of the formation of the State. One is seen here in typical rugged surroundings. (EGGED Historical Archive)

ABOVE RIGHT: D650HS 25651-60, BROCKHOUSE (SA), C37F
Two of ten long-wheelbase coaches new to South African Airways in 1957.

TJ 148–828, BROCKHOUSE (SA), C18CT
While not fully documented, this was thought to have been built around 1957 as well. South African Railways Road Transport Service operated a large fleet of passenger vehicles, including this coach with a similar body, but with only 18 seats in a 2 + 1 configuration, plus catering facilities and a toilet for tourists. Several other Freeline chassis were exported to South Africa and fitted with bus bodies, as were those to Australia and New Zealand. Others went to Belgium and Norway, where most were bodied as buses, although a few became coaches. (Both digitally coloured by Garry Luck from low-res scans which affect quality)

D650HS 25708, TCE 400, PLAXTON Consort II, (2330), C41F
New to Burwell & District Motor Service in July 1958. The chassis cost £2,534 and the body £2,712. This was the first Freeline coach for the home market to have the door ahead of the front wheels and the first with air-operated brakes and gear-change, although these features had been available for some time and were fitted to many exported chassis. It was withdrawn from service in 1972 and scrapped in August 1974. (Author)

D650HS 25713, UVE 101, PLAXTON Panorama, (592630), C41F
New to Burwell & District in June 1959, this was the last in a long line of Daimler coaches for this Cambridgeshire operator. The author was fortunate enough to drive this coach several times in its twilight years, which were extended by the acquisition of older Freelines (pages 53 and 61) that donated their vital organs to keep the old girl going but it was eventually scrapped in August 1974. Seen here before delivery inside the Daimler works at Coventry, outside the showroom building that displayed the Royal Warrant. (The Bus Archive, digitally coloured by Garry Luck)

G6HS 25712, XRW 403, WILLOWBROOK Viking, (59392), C41F
New to Coventry Corporation in May 1959, this is the last one of fleet numbers 401–3, seen here behind Harnall Lane garage in March 1967. The three Freelines had been re-painted sky blue/white with COVENTRY CITY TRANSPORT fleet names to match Duple-bodied Bedford coaches that had joined the Private Hire fleet. Displaced from front-line duties by the light-weight coaches, they were fitted with driver operated folding doors and a luggage pen replaced the front double seat to make them more suitable for stage carriage work. The trio were withdrawn and offered for tender in 1970 and sold to operators in Liverpool. (John Boylett, digitally coloured by Garry Luck)

G6HS 25710, XRW 401, WILLOWBROOK Viking, (59391), C41F
Built to replace Brush-bodied CVD6 single-deck buses that had dual-purpose seats for Private Hire, the combination of a Gardner engine and low-ratio differential made them unsuitable for efficient travel on motorways. For example, if one of these coaches had left Pool Meadow in Coventry bound for London at the same time as a Midland Red motorway express coach, the Midland Red would probably have passed the Daimler in the opposite direction on the M1 on its return journey. The maroon roof indicates the third livery of these coaches, re-painted for stage carriage work as seen here in Pool Meadow Bus Station. The original livery with cream roof can be seen on the front cover. (Tom Moore Collection)

D650HS 25072, XWX 912, PLAXTON Consort IV, (592665), C41C
New to W Pyne & Sons, Starbeck, Harrogate, Yorkshire in July 1959, this had the honour of becoming the last Daimler-engined coach to enter service in the UK. This centre-entrance coach had narrowly beaten front-entrance examples 120 JRB and UVE 101, which had both entered service the previous month. The chassis of XWX 912 had been new in 1953 and used by Daimler for experimental purposes. This unique coach was acquired by James Rowell, Prudhoe, Northumberland in January 1967. (Richard Simons)

D650HS 25709, 120 JRB, BURLINGHAM Seagull VII, (6753), C37F
New to Tailby & George, (Blue Bus Services), Willington, Derbyshire, fleet no. Dr 18 in June 1959. The chassis cost £2,532 and the body £2,825, seen here behind the depot at Willington. It was withdrawn in July 1972 and sold to a group of enthusiasts from Croydon in Surrey, who also owned PRA 388, a former Blue Bus Daimler CD650 double-decker. They both attended several bus rallies and events. The coach was eventually abandoned and finished up at Hoyle`s scrapyard in Barnsley by December 1983. It was then rescued by Dean Lomax of Hyde, Cheshire in 1984 and has since passed through several preservationist owners and is still awaiting restoration. (Author)

G6HS 25721, FEX 123, ROE, (GO5360), DP43F
New to Great Yarmouth Corporation Transport Department, fleet no. 23 in January 1962. Although not strictly classed as coaches, the dual-purpose seats, overhead luggage racks and rear boot made these vehicles suitable for medium distance journeys on hire to various coach operators in the summer period, either as a relief or replacement for breakdowns. Their main use was as one-person operated local buses. (Roy Marshall, The Bus Archive)

G6HS 25722, FEX 524, ROE, (GO5410), DP43F
New to Great Yarmouth Corporation, fleet no. 24 in January 1962. It was specified to match the Gardner engine and Daimatic transmission of recently purchased double-deckers by the legendary general manager, Geoffrey Hilditch, with a lowered driving position to provide an acceptable entrance height. He was well known within the industry for his choice of unusual vehicles. Four of the batch of five (FEX 122–3, 524–5) survived until 1977 when FEX 122 was converted to a mobile workshop/tow truck that served the Corporation until September 1986. (Cliff Essex)

G6HS 25725, AEX 19B, ROE, (GO5802), DP43F
Three more dual-purpose Freelines arrived at Great Yarmouth in 1964, registered JEX 418–20, fleet nos. 18–20, entering service as AEX 18–20B. They featured Alexander-style wrap-around windscreens, making them look more coach-like than the previous five. The second, No. 19, was painted in a revised livery of predominantly cream in 1966 to mark the tenth anniversary of the twinning of Great Yarmouth with the French town of Rambouillet. The white headrest covers and destination indicate that 'Rambouillet' had travelled south on a Private Hire and parked in the depot of Southend Corporation Transport in April 1967. (Paul Bateson)

G6HS 25724, AEX 18B, ROE, (GO5800), DP43F
The Great Yarmouth Freelines were withdrawn by the end of 1977, half going to Barnsley dealer Ken Askin, who sold AEX 18–20B to Omnibus Promotions in a dealer capacity in May 1978. They then passed to the varied fleet of Edwards, Joys Green, Lydbrook, Gloucestershire, who were part of Paul Tizard, (Holdings), as seen here on an enthusiast visit in June 1979. All three went to Paul Sykes at Barnsley in November 1979. (Terry Walker)

FAKE FREELINES?

During the early 1960s, Transport Vehicles (Daimler) Ltd. and Guy Motors both came under the ownership of the Jaguar Group, resulting in examples of "Badge Engineering" to meet the needs of certain export markets where brand loyalty had been built up over the years. Daimler Freelines had proved popular in Portugal, so when CCFL (Lisbon Electric Tramways Ltd.) required some in 1967, the order was met by mechanically similar Guy Victory UF chassis built at Wolverhampton, allocated Guy chassis numbers but badged as Daimlers and classified CVU6LX, indicating Gardner engines. Twenty-six chassis were supplied in 1967, 20 with UTIC B18T bus bodies and six as C41F coaches as seen here. (Lawrence Murphy)

The reverse situation arose in the same year when a Belgian customer wanted rear-engined Guys. Four Daimler Roadliners were supplied to SNCV with Jonckheere B46D bodies, badged as Guy Conquests and allocated Daimler chassis numbers 36154–7. Also badged as a Guy Conquest was a unique double-deck coach with CH38/32D Irizar bodywork built on chassis number 36125 for Madrivision of Spain in 1972 (page 92).

CHAPTER 3
REAR-ENGINED

Even before the last G6HS Freelines had been built, Daimler experimental engineers were busy developing a rear-engined single-deck chassis to take advantage of the increased permitted maximum length from 30 to 36ft. Two prototype chassis were constructed, designated SRD6 (36000–1), with a horizontal turbocharged CD6 8.6 litre engine mounted transversely at the rear. Power was transmitted through a fluid flywheel, and epicyclic semi-automatic gearbox and right-angle drive to the rear axle, as in the Fleetline double-decker. One was shown on the Daimler stand at the 1962 Commercial Motor Show at Earls Court to gauge operators' reactions, but neither were bodied.

Takeovers and mergers have often affected the choice of components in vehicles and, as part of the Jaguar Group, Daimler found that a V-formation engine mounted in-line between the chassis members might be more practical, providing a straight transmission line forward from the engine, through the gearbox to the rear axle, eliminating the need for an angle drive. Daimler had designed and built V8 petrol engines for their limousines and sports cars, so were familiar with the concept. If Daimler had remained an independent company and developed a V8 diesel engine, then the Roadliner story may have been different! Due to the links between the Jaguar Group and American-owned Cummins engines, the 9.6 litre Cummins V6-200 was chosen. Air suspension was standard, with a further choice of Metalastik rubber suspension or steel leaf springs.

A prototype SRD6 show chassis. (Official Daimler photo)

LEFT: Development continued with the next three chassis, designated CRC6, indicating the fitting of a Cummins V6 engine. All three were eventually bodied as buses, 35002 as a demonstrator, 36003 for Potteries Motor Traction and 36004 was exported to Edmonton Transit System in Canada. Duple Motor bodies supplied an artist`s impression of their Commander body, which was used in advertisements in the trade press.

OPPOSITE: SRC6 36005, DUPLE Commander, (1195/1), C49F
This was the first Roadliner chassis to carry a coach body. It was exhibited on the Duple (Northern) stand at the 1964 Commercial Motor Show at Earls Court. Fitted with a front-mounted radiator and air suspension, it was registered as CWK 641C in 1965. The real thing is a good likeness to the impression, as seen here in a Daimler publicity photo taken in typical Cotswold surroundings. (Official Daimler photo, digitally coloured by Garry Luck)

Rear-Engined

ABOVE LEFT and ABOVE RIGHT: CWK 641C was kept busy as a demonstrator providing road tests for the trade press and used in service by coach operators who were potential customers. Two potential orders were probably lost on Saturday 27 July 1966 when Flight`s Coaches was using it on their express service from Birmingham to Great Yarmouth and it broke down on the A11, near Elveden in Suffolk. The Daimler service department asked Burwell & District if they could recover it to their depot, which was achieved by a length of chain attached to Daimler Freeline LCE 800. Daimler engineers travelled to Burwell on the following Monday, well prepared with a spare Cummins engine strapped to their Fleetline test chassis. The coach was repaired and driven back to Coventry, but Burwell & District cancelled their order for a new Roadliner. Flight`s did not place an order, instead purchasing a Plaxton-bodied Bristol RELH, JON 700E, which was entered in the 1967 British Coach Rally at Brighton, where it was judged Best Standard Coach. If Flight`s had chosen the Roadliner, Daimler and Plaxton may have pulled off a triple win at Brighton, instead of the double honours achieved by KDD 276E and LAP 665E. (Left: Author; Right: Paul Bateson)

RIGHT: Further appearances of CWK 641C were made in the demonstration park at Earls Court in September 1966 and at the Duple Group Show at Hendon in October 1965 and 1967, when the Author enjoyed several demonstration rides along the Edgware Road. (Author)

ABOVE LEFT: CWK 641C was sold to Red House Motor Services, Coventry in May 1969. It did finally reach Great Yarmouth where it is seen here in the Beach Coach Station, on 11 July 1970. (Author)

ABOVE RIGHT: Closer to home, it is about to depart from Pool Meadow, Coventry. The names of the constituent companies 'BANTAM-BTS-BUNTY-GODIVA-RHMS' were carried on the sides of coaches until replaced by 'RED HOUSE GROUP' by the new owners of Red House, who introduced a revised livery as seen in the third picture. (DJ Little)

RIGHT: It was withdrawn in 1976 and scrapped locally in Coventry, where it had spent most of its life. (Tom Moore, digitally coloured by Garry Luck)

SRC6 36104, HDG 772D, PLAXTON Panorama I, (673450), C47F, Fleet no.272
The first of 38 Roadliners for Black & White Motorways, Cheltenham was displayed on the Daimler stand at the 1966 Commercial Motor Show at Earls Court. Although retaining the D suffix registration, it did not enter service until March 1967. It was one of the first Roadliners to be retro-fitted with a Perkins V8-510 engine in an attempt to improve reliability in 1968. Seen here at Cardiff Bus Station in September 1973. (Mike Street)

As part of the National Bus Company, Black & White was required to comply with the corporate white livery as seen here at Cheltenham Coach Station. The unique Daimler badge, which was a cut-down version of the fluted winged emblem, remained in place from new to final owner. When National Travel (South West) was formed in 1973, it was re-numbered 172 and then finally withdrawn in November 1975, passing to a dealer in Macclesfield. After a couple of subsequent owners, it made the final journey to Joe Sykes' scrapyard at Barnsley in September 1982. (Author`s collection)

SRC6 36121, KDD 276E, PLAXTON Panorama I, (673454), C44F, Fleet no. 276
This was the only one of a batch of seven (KDD 273–5, 7–9E were C47F) to have reclining seats. It is seen here entering the North Promenade to take part in the National Coach Rally at Blackpool on 2 April 1967, where it was awarded the Coach of the Year cup, Plaxton Trophy and Class Concours winner. Prizes were awarded by the Mayor of Blackpool who attended in his official limousine, a Daimler Majestic Major, registration FV 1, powered by a V8 petrol engine, which was parked beside the pair of prizewinning Daimler coaches for the presentation. (John Kaye)

KDD 276E repeated the success of Blackpool in the British Coach Rally at Brighton two weeks later, winning the Coach of the Year, Plaxton Trophy and Brighton Trophy. 'The Black Knight' once again taking second place, despite the more luxurious specification, which put it in a different class for judging. A third Cummins-engined coach entered in the same rally was a heavily modified Plaxton-bodied Ford R226, driven by owner Don Janes, who had specified that an Allison automatic gearbox be attached to the front-mounted Cummins V8 engine for his Whitefriars Coaches fleet. (John Kaye)

KDD 273–9E were withdrawn in 1971 and soon found new owners with independent coach operators. KDD 277E and 279E were acquired by 'Paddy' Harris, (International Progressive Coachline), Cambridge in August 1971, who added another double seat. They both passed to Kuehnlenze, (Ernie`s Coaches), Upper Langwith, Derbyshire in 1975, who ran them for a while. KDD 277E is seen here parked at a refreshment stop in Essex on the way to an east coast resort in September 1971. (Geoff Mills)

KDD 278E changed hands frequently, initially going to Homer & Jones, Quarry Bank in August 1971, passing to Richards, Chilton Trinity in December 1973, and then to Patel, Leicester in August 1974. The final operator was George Dack of Terrington St Clement in Norfolk in December 1977. Seen here at the Kings Lynn Bus Rally in September 1981, it was withdrawn with suspension trouble in September 1985, eventually passing to a fellow Roadliner operator for spares, and then scrapped. (Geoff Mills)

SRC6 36125, M-1979-D, IRIZAR, CH38/32D
This chassis was exported to Spanish agent SACIA in 1967, and designs were invited for a suitable double-decker sightseeing coach from Irizar and Ayats. The Irizar design was chosen, and the unique double-decker was built in 1971, entering the Madrivision fleet of Autopullman SA, Madrid as a Guy Conquest in March 1972. Seen here at the depot in July 1982, awaiting repairs to the air-conditioning system which was essential on this coach. (Ian Charlton)

SRC6 36025, TCD 1161, MOTOR BODY ASSEMBLERS, C39FT
Daimler and Guy were under common ownership of the Jaguar group and had premises in South Africa, where one of a pair of locally bodied luxury coaches fitted with toilets for Atlas Tours, Johannesburg, South Africa is seen here when new in 1967. Although a good number of Roadliners were exported to South Africa, most were buses. A third coach went to Springs Municipality in 1968. (Official Daimler photo, digitally coloured by Garry Luck)

SRC6 36127, MDH 212E, PLAXTON Panorama I, (673462), C51F
This is the second of a pair new to Central Coachways, Walsall in May 1967, who were a subsidiary of the Walsall Co-operative Society, until sold to West Midlands Travel in 1984. Central had previously purchased three Duple-bodied Freelines in 1955 (page 50–1). (Author)

The pair were disposed of to dealer W S Yeates of Loughborough by the end of 1970. MDH 212E was sold to Croft Coaches, Cardiff in April 1971, as seen here, who ran it for a year and then returned it to Yeates, who sold it to G H Nash, Nuneaton. After a while, it finished up as a café in Nuneaton bus station. (Glen Bubb, Colour Classics)

OPPOSITE: SRC6 36152, KVT 198E, PLAXTON Panorama I, (673459), C49F
One of three coaches new to Potteries Motor Traction, Stoke-on-Trent, (KVT 197–9E, fleet nos. C1097–9) in May 1967. Great Yarmouth Beach Coach Station was the destination of a regular long cross-country journey from Staffordshire in August 1967. The open luggage lockers reveal the capacity for holiday-makers' suitcases. Previously, visiting coaches caused congestion on the seafront at arrival and departure times, with consequent disruption to local bus services. The former Midland & Great Northern Railway closed in 1959 and the beach terminus station was acquired by the Corporation. General manager Geoffrey Hilditch masterminded the change from accommodating passenger vehicles with steel wheels to those fitted with rubber tyres in the form of motor coaches, retaining some of the original platforms by 1961. More than 60 coach operators were licensed by the Corporation Transport Department, who ran the operation to use the new facility. Busy summer Saturdays like this would see several of the Corporation Daimler Freelines on standby with spare drivers available to cope with any overloads to most parts of the country. PMT operated a large fleet of Roadliner buses and bought two trios of coaches, but they proved unreliable. (Author)

TOP RIGHT and BOTTOM RIGHT: KVT 199E passed to B Smith & T G Coward, (Travellers Friend), Blackpool in August 1973 and is seen here in May 1975 (top right), on the premises of Brian Kellett, (Border Tours), Barnoldswick, Lancashire, before it was re-painted in to their standard livery, entering service in August 1975 (lower right). Border Tours also ran a pair of ex Black & White Roadliners, NAD 291–2F (page 109). (Top: Terry Walker; bottom: Author's Collection)

SRC6 36158, LAP 665E, PLAXTON Panorama I, (673463), C27F
Seven double and six single reclining seats gave this coach 20 forward facing seats, in addition to a curved settee for five and two swivel seats at the rear. It also provided a seat for the hostess, who could serve hot or cold drinks from the bar which was equipped with twin coffee percolators and a fridge. Surprisingly for such a high-specification coach, which included power-operated roof lights and fold-down steps to the rear emergency door, no toilet was fitted. New to Woburn Garage, (Evan Evans Tours), London WC1 as 'The Black Night' in April 1967, it entered the National Coach Rally at Blackpool in April, where it was awarded runner-up to Coach of the Year and class Concours winner. (John Kaye)

RIGHT: Once again, it came runner-up to Black & White KDD 276E at the British Coach Rally at Brighton. The curved rear seating can be seen in this view. (Author)

BELOW RIGHT: Evan Evans sold out to Wallace Arnold in February 1969, who re-painted the coach in their grey livery with additional Evan Evans names. The troublesome Cummins V6 engine was replaced by a Perkins V8.510 unit in 1970 and was later up-seated to carry 47 passengers. (Andrew Harvey-Adams)

BELOW LEFT: Withdrawn in October 1972, it passed to dealer Stanley Hughes, who sold it to J Illes, (Aireborough Coach Tours), Rawdon, Yorkshire in October 1973. It then passed, in damaged condition, to Bernard Rees, (Lands End Coaches), St Just, Cornwall in May 1976, who repaired and ran it successfully until a handbrake malfunction caused it to roll over a cliff at Mousehole in January 1978. Although the Perkins engine was still running, the coach was written off. (David Stanier)

SRC6 36159-61, PLAXTON Panorama I, (673464-6), C49FT

Three of these coaches were exported to MacNab Bus Sales, Ingersoll, Ontario, Canada in 1967. Originally specified with only 40 seats, tables and servery, it appears from photos that they left these shores with 49 seats and a toilet at the rear. The width was reduced to 8ft to comply with Canadian regulations, which further required a spring handbrake, a fire alarm system for the engine compartment and two push-out windows on each side. They were also fitted with power steering and a second alternator. The first coach was shipped in June 1967, with the other two following in December of that year. (Official Daimler photo, digitally coloured by Garry Luck)

RIGHT: The first of this trio carried license plate 123 OBU with Grant Coach Lines, Ontario when seen here at Toronto City Hall in June 1975. (Paul Bateson)

BELOW LEFT: The second was sold to Lance Vough and subsequently extensively rebuilt mechanically, first with a Deutz V8 air-cooled diesel engine, followed by a John Deere tractor engine by owner Joe Roukens when converted into a motorhome. It is seen here while registered as 119 SCB at Bronte Creek 'British Car Day' in September 2003. The small JOHN DEERE emblem can be seen above the DAIMLER badge. (Paul Bateson)

BELOW RIGHT: The third is seen here at Kitchener, Ontario in May 1982, also converted into a motorhome. Appropriately it was named 'Its A Family Affair' and registered RKL 444 at the time. (Paul Bateson)

SRC6 36164, PLAXTON Panorama I, (673469), C51F
This was the last of six left-hand drive chassis bodied by Plaxton in 1967 with consecutive chassis and body numbers. The first three went to Canada (pages 100–1), the fourth and fifth were exported to Switzerland without seats which were fitted locally. The sixth coach, seen here in a sales brochure, went to Poland and no further ownership details are known, apart from the initial dealer, Motoimport. (Daimler brochure)

SRC6 36257, KWK 220F, PLAXTON Panorama I, (689354), C35F
New to Red House Motor Services, Coventry in October 1967. The low seating capacity indicated additional luxury features to the order of Coventry City FC, for which it served as the team coach until Red House lost the contract, when seating capacity was increased to 49. Joined by ex-demonstrator CWK 641C (pages 83–5) in May 1969, the pair of Roadliners did not have far to return to the Daimler service depot at Kingfield Road in Coventry for subsequent warranty repairs and eventual replacement of their troublesome Cummins engines by more reliable Perkins V8 units. It was withdrawn in June 1976 and sold to Don Everall, dealer, and scrapped a year later. (Alan Snatt)

SRC6 36024, TNU 687F, PLAXTON Panorama I, (683470), C51F
New to Tailby & George, (Blue Bus Services), fleet no. Dr 25, Willington, Derbyshire in September 1967. The low chassis number indicates that this was one of the first Roadliner coaches to be ordered by this loyal Daimler customer. Blue Bus had operated most types of the marque over the years and may have been unique in having CVD6, Freeline and Roadliner coaches in service at the same time. Despite meticulous maintenance and sympathetic drivers, this coach still suffered mechanical problems common to other Roadliners. (Author)

Blue Bus Services were sold to Derby Corporation in December 1973. TNU 687F was re-numbered 40 in the municipal fleet which became Derby Borough Transport on 1 April 1974. In September 1974 it was re-painted in Derby Larkspur blue/cream but then returned to traditional Blue Bus colours with Derby crest and fleet names before re-entering service, as seen here. Sadly, this coach was one of 19 vehicles destroyed in the depot fire on 5 January 1976. (D Taylor, Nottingham Heritage Vehicles Collection)

SRC6 36196, PVT 100F, DUPLE (Northern) Commander III, (188/1), C49F
The first of three Duple-bodied Roadliners with consecutive chassis, body and registration numbers new to Potteries Motor Traction, Stoke-on-Trent in March 1968, fleet numbers C1100–2. Seen here at Blackpool in September 1968. It was sold to Campings Coaches, Brighton in June 1972, passing to Blue Line, Upminster, a year later and then onto two other operators in the London area. (Author)

SRC6 36197, PVT 101F, DUPLE (Northern) Commander III, (188/2), C49F
The six Roadliner coaches' lives with PMT were brief, and they were advertised for sale by a dealer in September 1971. PVT 101F also went to Campings Coaches, Brighton in June 1972 but soon passed to Phillips Coaches, Dormston, Worcestershire in May 1973. It was sold to Alan Jeynes (Malvern Hills Coach Hire) in May 1977 and then sold for scrap in April 1979. (Andrew Harvey-Adams, digitally altered by Garry Luck)

SRC6 36271, NAD 297F, PLAXTON Panorama I, (689362), C47F
New to Black & White Motorways, Cheltenham in June 1968. One of a batch of ten (NAD 290–9F), the coach is seen here approaching Victoria Coach Station, London in August 1968. Unusually for Plaxton, the registration numbers were not consecutive with chassis numbers, but the body numbers were. (Alan Snatt)

None of the Cummins-engined Black & White Roadliners received all-over white National livery, so not all subsequent owners re-painted them. Brian Kellett, (Border Tours), Barnoldswick, Lancashire acquired NAD 291F in May 1973, moved the number plate to a more conventional position and added Daimler and Cummins badges as seen here at Battersea Wharf coach park in London in September 1975. He also acquired NAD 292F, which had passed through three other owners in the meantime. Both coaches passed to T M Roach of Truro, Cornwall in July 1977. (Ian Charlton)

SRC6 36293, ULR 963F, DUPLE (Northern) Commander III, (188/4), C30F
This was the second 'Executive' Roadliner for Evan Evans Tours, London. It entered service in June 1968 and was known as 'Quicksilver', finished in anodized ribbed aluminium which did not quite match the finish of the painted fibreglass front panel. There were 22 reclining seats in pairs, plus seating for eight more around a curved table at the rear. Unusually, a drinks servery and wardrobe were fitted at the front of the coach, and a video TV screen was mounted above. Costing around £15,000, Gwyn Evans announced at the Trade launch that he expected to take delivery of three more similar vehicles, but they were cancelled. (Cliff Essex)

Evans Transport Enterprises catered for an up-market clientele and no doubt the Daimler chassis was chosen more for prestige than reliability. They sold out to Wallace Arnold in February 1969 in what turned out to be one of their less profitable acquisitions. 'Quicksilver' retained original livery, engine and interior layout until withdrawal in November 1972, when it passed to dealer Stanley Hughes. It was sold to Alan McKenzie, (County Coaches), Clydebank, Scotland, in July 1973, and then back south to I S Scott, Canterbury in August 1975, where its unique specification was utilised as a band bus for Woody Woodmansey`s U Boat, a seventies rock band. It is seen here at Wivenhoe in Essex in November 1976. (Geoff Mills)

SRC6 36202, KKV 800G, PLAXTON Derwent II, (689465), DP53F
With an experimental chassis built in 1967 and converted to SRP8 with Perkins 8.36 litre V8-510 engine, it was bodied and registered in September 1968 for display in the demonstration park at Earls Court. Although this is not a coach, the dual-purpose seating makes it eligible for inclusion in the same way as the Great Yarmouth Freelines (pages 76–9). The underfloor luggage lockers also made it suitable for coach work. Daimler engineers were aware of the problems with the Cummins V6 engines fitted to previous Roadliners, so had experimented with an alternative engine. Although tried in service by several operators, no new orders were generated. (Grahame Wareham)

ABOVE LEFT: KKV 800G was sold to City of Oxford Motor Services in March 1970 and given fleet no. 639. It is seen here in their traditional livery on an enthusiast visit to Stoke-on-Trent in July 1970, in company with a native PMT Marshall-bodied Roadliner bus. The former demonstrator was no stranger to the Potteries as it had been on hire to PMT the previous year. (Grahame Wareham)

ABOVE RIGHT: By May 1973, it was re-painted in South Midland livery and re-numbered 18. (Grahame Wareham)

RIGHT: The final re-paint was into standard NBC poppy red/white dual-purpose livery in 1974. It was withdrawn in July 1975 and driven to Barraclough`s Scrapyard at Carlton, Yorkshire the next year. (Richard Simons)

SRP8 36299, RDG 305G, PLAXTON Panorama Elite, (693356), C47F
One of the first batch of ten (RDG 300–9G) to be fitted with steel leaf springs instead of Metalastik rubber suspension and a Perkins V8-510 instead of Cummins V6 engine. New to Black & White Motorways, Cheltenham in June 1969. Plaxton were able to match the body and registration numbers to the chassis numbers, unlike the previous batch! RDG 305G, seen here, approaches Gloucester Green Bus Station, Oxford, still in traditional livery on the way home to Cheltenham in 1972. (Grahame Wareham)

SRP8 36300, RDG 306G, PLAXTON Panorama Elite, (693357), C47F
Several coaches from this batch were painted in National Travel, (South West) corporate coach livery of white, with a broad waistband in the colour relevant to the name of the constituent company in 1970. This small acknowledgement to identity was swept away by an overall white **NATIONAL** livery with small red fleet names in 1972, as carried here by RDG 306G departing from Cheltenham Coach Station in September 1974. (Alan Snatt)

Twenty-one Perkins-engined Roadliners were withdrawn by Black & White in November 1975 and replaced by older underfloor-engined coaches. They were sold to dealer Transport (Passenger Equipment) Limited, Macclesfield, who re-sold them to gullible independent coach operators who thought they were getting a bargain! RDG 305G, 306G, and 308G went to T W Stanton, (B Cabs), Blythe Bridge, Staffordshire in 1976. RDG 305G and 308G later went to Aytons, Nantwich, Cheshire in August 1977, who then sold them both to A J & N M Carr, Charing Heath, Kent. RDG 308G entered service in January 1983, while 305G provided spares. (Martyn Hearson)

RDG 309G had the distinction of being loaned to Grey Cars from September 1969 to May 1970 and was equipped with tables and a bar to serve as team coach for Torquay United Football Club for the season, carrying the grey band in corporate style of the time. After initial sale by the dealer, it passed through the hands of several operators in the Sheffield area, including J W Briddock, (Charnock Coaches), who ran it for almost three years, as seen here. (Richard Simons)

SRP8 36316, RAR 677H, PLAXTON Panorama Elite, (709462), C51F
New to Carlo Inzani, London in June 1970. Evan Evans must have been pleased with the Black Knight and Quicksilver, as they ordered three more Roadliner SRP8 chassis with Duple bodies, with an option on two more. This would have doubled the number of Duple-bodied Roadliners built but, when Wallace Arnold took over Evan Evans, the order was cancelled. Three chassis were built and bodied by Plaxton for Arlington Motors to sell. The other two chassis (36318–9) were not built. RAR 677H returned to Arlington in July 1972 and was sold to Yeardley, Mosborough, Yorkshire in March 1973. In November 1974, it was sold to Martin, Penicuick, Scotland. (John Kaye)

ABOVE LEFT: SRP8 36315, EWA 219H, PLAXTON Panorama Elite, (709461), C53F
One of the three chassis cancelled by Evan Evans was supplied through Arlington Motors to Eric H Sims, Sheffield, Yorkshire in April 1970. Sims was an old established operator and had previously bought a new Plaxton-bodied Daimler CVD6 coach in 1949. (Author)

ABOVE RIGHT: Sims was probably not impressed with the Roadliner, as it was sold by the end of the year, to be acquired by Carwise, London W2 in March 1971, and is seen here in Oxford. (Grahame Wareham)

RIGHT: Three years later it crossed the Severn Bridge into South Wales to join the fleet of Williams, Cwmdu, and then to John Richards, Nantyglo in January 1975, who later also added a pair of ex Black & White Roadliners, (RDG 300G and 303G). It is seen here at Blackpool in October 1979. (Terry Walker)

SRP8 36334, UAD 310H, PLAXTON Panorama Elite, (709451), C47F
The final batch of Roadliners for Black & White Motorways (UAD 310–9H) also had consecutive chassis, body and registration numbers and were new in May 1970. They were also the last vehicles to be delivered in traditional Black & White livery with stainless steel fleet names above the front wheels below window level. Here, UAD 310H takes a break in Oxford's Gloucester Green Bus Station in 1972. (Grahame Wareham)

SRP8 36339, UAD 315H, PLAXTON Panorama Elite, (709456)
In line with the rest of the fleet, this coach was re-painted in **NATIONAL** livery and re-numbered 215. It also retained the stainless-steel BLACK & WHITE MOTORWAYS fleet name, unlike RDG 306G (page 115) which carried the fleet name in red in the NBC corporate style. (Richard Simons)

Due to the poor reputation of Daimler Roadliners, rumour at the time was that dealers were offering a buy two get one free offer on them, as several operators had bought trios. Stapleford of Markfield, Leicestershire, bought UAD 310H, 311H, and 313H in December 1975 and labelled them 'ROADLINER No.1–3'. They must have liked them as they also bought UAD 318H from B A Garratt, Leicester, in May 1977, labelling it 'ROADLINER No.4'. Staplefords also liked Commer 2-stroke engines, fitting one in UAD 313H linked to a manual gearbox. (Martyn Hearson)

Max McSorley from Eardington, near Bridgnorth, Shropshire also bought three Roadliners, RDG 300G, UAD 315H and 319H in February 1976. He put green stripes on the white coachwork but did not keep them long. UAD 319H headed north via Fletcher, Marple, Cheshire, in April 1977, then to L E Pringle, (Fiesta Coaches), Swarland, Northumberland, in September 1977, and arriving with H E Craiggs, at nearby Amble in August 1979, but it did not enter service until January 1980. (D J Little)

Daimler Coaches in Colour

OPPOSITE: SRP8 36317, RAR 678H, PLAXTON Panorama Elite, (709463), C51F
The third cancelled Evan Evans chassis bodied by Plaxton was registered in a long consecutive series by Arlington as dealers and purchased by Best & Sons, Ealing, London W5 before the August plate date change but continued to carry an H-suffix until at least 26 September 1970, when John Kaye captured the rear end while parked in Abingdon Street, Westminster. The extensive air vents are apparent on the rear of the body and the art of the signwriter is clearly displayed, as was common before the days of vinyl lettering. (John Kaye)

ABOVE RIGHT: On Sunday, 20 September 1970, the Author travelled to London in his Daimler Conquest Century car, ready to visit the Commercial Motor Show at Earls Court the next day. Knowing of the delivery of this coach, he called at the home of Alec Best, at Priory Gardens, on the off-chance of seeing it. Maybe Alec was impressed by the Daimler car, but he looked at his watch and said, 'If we are quick, we might just catch it'. He was quick, as his Shelby Cobra Mustang car whizzed down to the West End, where he proudly showed the Author his latest coach, still bearing the original number plate, RAR 678H. (Author)

Best & Sons were regular entrants in the British Coach Rally and were well known for unusual vehicles, having entered a Whitson-bodied Sentinel in the first rally at Clacton in 1955, where Ron Best won the road section and driving test. The Roadliner was a one-off for Best but they later ran the unique V8-engined AEC Sabre, which was of similar layout to a Roadliner. By the time the Author saw the same coach at the next Brighton Coach Rally in April 1971, the H-suffix on the number plate had been changed to J to rectify the discrepancy. (Author)

SRP8 36317
RAR 678J was entered in the National Coach Rally at Blackpool in April 1971 and a week later went to Brighton, where the puff of smoke from the exhaust seen here indicates that driver Alec Best may have been putting his foot down during the driving tests on Madeira Drive. If only we could hear the crackle of the Perkins V8 engine! The Best brothers were regular rally entrants and Alec was often a class winner in driving tests, despite a broken leg one year. (Alan Snatt)

RIGHT: RAR 678J passed to Ron Hutchinson, (Ivy Taxis), Linthwaite, Yorkshire in April 1973, where it stayed until May 1975 when it was acquired by Rigby, Patricroft and seen here at Fleetwood in October that year. (Ian Charlton)

BELOW RIGHT: The next brief Welsh owners were J Nicholls, Tredegar, and J Crookes, Cardiff. It moved north to Beric Hardman, Waterfoot, Lancashire in February 1978 who painted it black and white and then sold to Hugo Miller, (Arun Coaches), Horsham, Sussex, in December 1978, where it is seen here in April 1979. (Author)

BELOW LEFT: The next move was back up north to Carl Green, (Carlton Coaches of Halifax), Luddendenfoot, Yorkshire in June 1979. The Mixenden Crowns Jazz Band were the last passengers to be carried before the final journey to Barnsley in 1985. (Terry Walker)

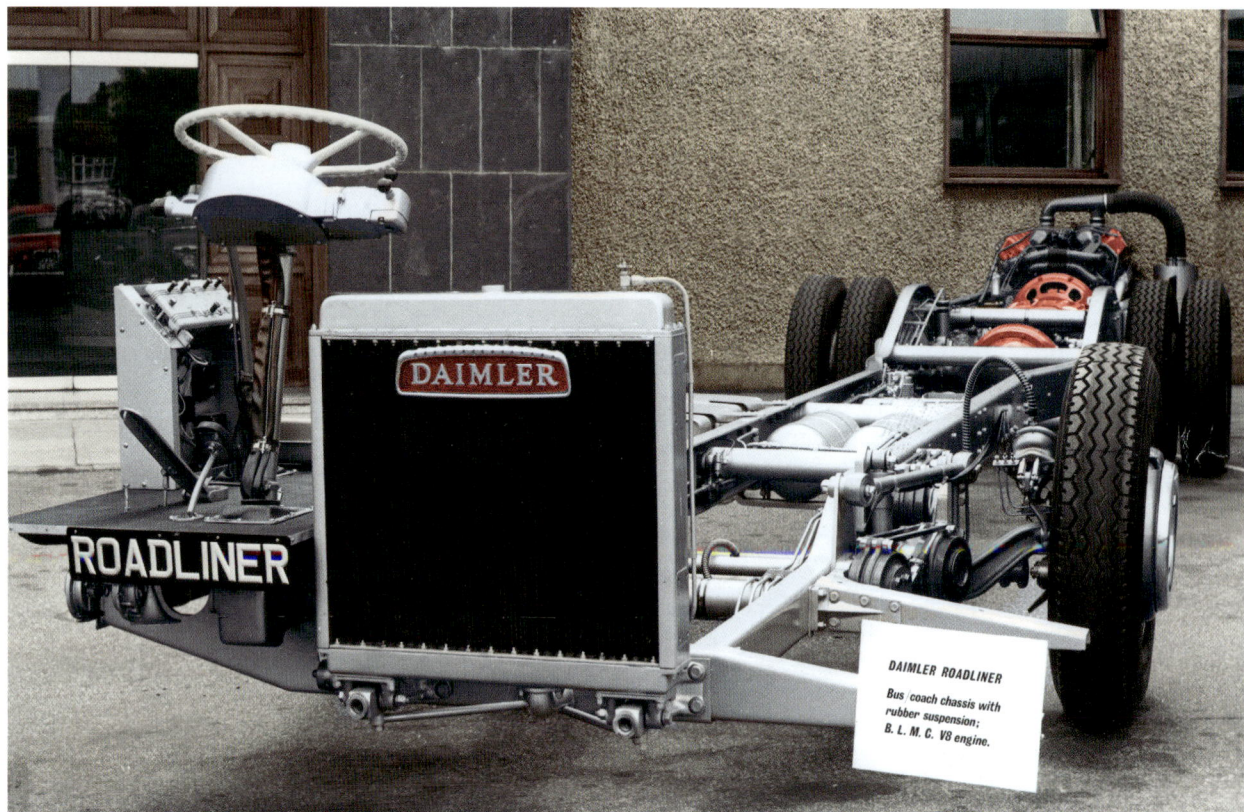

SRL8 36304
This was an experimental chassis fitted with a 13.1 litre V8 engine, designed and developed by AEC and labelled BL-810. When exhibited as a show chassis at the 1969 Brussels Motor Show, it was badged as a Guy Conquest and as a Daimler Roadliner SRL8 at the Scottish Motor Show in Glasgow later that same year. The true potential for this powerful engine was never realised, due to political implications and the attitude of British Leyland management. They were intent on destroying the names of constituent companies but were themselves eventually killed off by Continental competitors. The chassis was reported to have passed to Black & White Motorways for spares in 1972. (Official Daimler photo, digitally coloured by Garry Luck)